Contents

'Paleo diet' is a phrase that is heard more than ever before as it increases in popularity. More and more people are realising the powerful positive impact the diet and lifestyle can have on their health… but what exactly is it?

The Origins of the Paleo Diet

The Paleo diet dates back to the last century. In 1975, the esteemed gastroenterologist Dr. Walter Voegtlin published his book, The Stone Age Diet. This explained how he treated patients with illnesses such as Crohn's disease and IBS with a diet that replicated the eating habits of people from the Paleolithic era. In essence, the diet comprised consuming large amounts of animal protein and fats and relatively tiny amounts of carbohydrates. The health of Dr. Voegtlin's patients was reported to have improved significantly.

Despite the documented proof of benefits, The Stone Age Diet did not really take off since the majority of people thought that a low-fat, low-calorie diet was the only healthy way to eat.

The following decade, in 1985, Dr. Stanley Boyd Eaton and Dr. Melvin Konner published research supporting Dr. Voegtlin's claims in a white paper that received huge press attention. They went on to publish The Paleolithic Prescription: A Program of Diet & Exercise and a Design for Living.

In the book, it is explained that our ancestors in the Paleolithic era, which started around 2.6 million years ago, ate an extremely healthy diet. The authors updated this diet and showed that the sample nutritional balance was available from many widely available modern foods. Their popular book set out many of the principles that founded today's Paleo diet.

It should be noted that there are different versions of diets that fall under the Paleo umbrella, each varying in degrees of strictness in the way that they follow the Paleolithic pattern. This is essentially a positive aspect as it involves a greater degree of choice, as you will learn in Chapter 3 when we look at the Paleo lifestyle. However, the Paleo diet described in this book adheres closely to the true principles of Paleo eating while remaining practical, modern and not unnecessarily restrictive, complicated or time-consuming. It really is the best way to start enjoying the highly beneficial Paleo diet and start enjoying the amazing results.

What the Paleo Diet Looks Like

The Paleo diet is based on a way of eating that pre-dates agriculture. This does not mean you have to start literally going out to hunt and gather your food (unless you really want to) – most people have busy lives and require an easy, fuss-free way to enjoy food every day. All the food in this book is readily available in farmers' markets, grocery stores and the healthier aisles of the supermarket.

Unlike the majority of diets recommended by Western food authorities; the Paleo diet inverts the standard food pyramid. So most of your calories come from eating meat, poultry, eggs, fish and seafood, followed by fats from plant foods, fruits and vegetables, and then nuts and seeds. This means that the Paleo diet is essentially high in protein and low in carbohydrates.

Chapter 2 details more about all the many foods you can eat, but for now you should just note that you will be eating no processed food or ready meals, limiting alcohol consumption, and eating no grains at all as they are agricultural foods – so no bread, rice, pasta etc., no legumes e.g. bean, peas and soy, and no added refined sugar.

Sound hard? Not at all – we provide all the information and recipes you will need here to get you going. Now read on as we explain just why you should choose to adopt the Paleo diet.

Its time to get started with Paleo - the diet that will transform your body, your health and of course, your life!

Chapter 1 - Why Choose Paleo?

At this stage you might say: "Sounds fine, but what is Paleo going to do for me?"

The short answer is – pretty much everything!

Paleo really is a phenomenally healthy way to live your life. The health benefits reach far and wide, so let's take a look at why eating this way helps your body to thrive.

Health Benefits of Paleo

Firstly, remember that on Paleo you are cutting out processed foods, alcohol, sugar, grains and legumes. It is only in the past several thousand years, or even in some case the past few decades, that we have started eating these things. The first of our species dates back over 6 million years, so even 10,000 years is just a blink of an eye. We have not evolved to eat these foodstuffs and our bodies do not need them. This is why we suffer the many modern "diseases of affluence" that afflict an increasing number of overweight people in the West. Paleo goes straight back to our super-healthy roots and cuts them all out. So what does that do for your body?

Paleo Helps Prevent Metabolic Syndrome
Metabolic syndrome is the term used to describe the group of risk factors which may lead to someone developing type 2 diabetes, stroke or heart disease. These risk factors include:

• A 40-inch waist for men, 35 inches for women

• Low HDL cholesterol (men under 40 mg/dL; women 50 mg/dL)

• High blood pressure (higher than 130/85 mm Hg)

• High triglycerides (higher than 150 mg/dL)

• High fasting blood sugar (higher than 100 mg/DL)

If three or more factors apply to someone, then they have metabolic syndrome.

The great news is that the Paleo diet can prevent or even reverse this dangerous state of affairs. It eliminates refined sugar, white flour and processed foods, plus it promotes eating lean proteins and healthy fats.

Paleo Improves Heart Health

Following the Paleo diet can greatly improve heart health. Since it recommends lean meats, fish and shellfish, all low in unhealthy saturated fats, it can help to lower bad cholesterol and triglycerides. Moreover it may be a key factor reducing or reversing arteriosclerosis, which is one of the primary causes of blood clots, stroke and aneurysms.

Paleo Aids Your Digestion

Who needs bread, really? The vast majority of processed grains and legumes, may have some role in triggering or worsening diseases such as coeliac disease, irritable bowel syndrome, Crohn's disease and so on. By cutting out wheat and other grains, plus eating fibrous foods such as fruit and vegetables, you will keep your digestive tract well-brushed and healthy. Many followers of the Paleo diet have not only lost weight, they have ceased to suffer from diarrhoea, constipation, flatulence, heartburn and other gastrointestinal discomforts.

Paleo Helps Fight Disease

Strengthen your immune system by supporting your body's defences. If you don't feed your body foods it was not designed to ingest, it will be better equipped to ward off allergies and other immune system issues like lupus and rheumatoid arthritis. In fact, sufferers of these ailments have reported that the Paleo diet has significantly improved their health.

Also, another huge benefit of the Paleo diet is that it is gluten- and lactose-free, plus it eliminates artificial additives, antibiotics, preservatives, hormones, colourings and other irritants. So, rather than have to fight off assaults from such unwanted ingredients, your body can fight disease. Many symptoms like headaches, nausea, bloating and other issues simply disappear – Paleo really is a win-win!

Of course, a huge health benefit can be weight loss, so keep reading to find out how Paleo can help you drop the pounds…

Chapter 2 - Foods for Your Paleo Plate

Fill Up Your Paleo Plate!

So far, we have looked a fair bit about what baddies you will be cutting out when you go Paleo. Now for the good stuff – what can you eat?

The short answer is LOTS!

Meats, Seafood and Eggs

These food will supply most of your calories. Every kind of unprocessed natural meat, fish, seafood and eggs are allowed, but for maximum benefits they will be wild, free range or organic. This is not compulsory as it is the more expensive path, but it will ensure you are getting the best quality nutrients.

Vegetable Fats

You can freely enjoy olives, olive oil, avocadoes (technically a fruit), nuts and seeds. Dairy products, like butter, are not used to cook but there are many great alternatives, listed later in this chapter.

Nuts and Seeds

Nuts were a huge part of Stone Age fare. All nuts are therefore allowed, with the exception of peanuts, which are in fact a legume. Seeds include flax, sunflower, pumpkin and sesame among others. Plus wonderful quinoa, a great alternative to pasta, rice and other grains.

Fruits and Vegetables

Go for it – enjoy any fruit that would have been foraged in the pre-agricultural era. This includes berries like cranberries, raspberries, strawberries and blueberries, plus tree fruits like citrus fruits, apples, plums, cherries, peaches and pears.

Root vegetables like potatoes and parsnips are too high in starch to be included but wild root vegetables are great as they can be foraged; see the list later in this chapter. You can also enjoy plenty of lettuce, leafy greens like spinach and kale, tomatoes, peppers, butternut squash, marrow and zucchini or courgette.

Condiments and Sauces

Certain condiments, like real mustard from seeds are allowed, but ketchup which is typically full of sugar, or soy sauce from legumes are not. Pure vinegar is permitted in small quantities, if it contains no additives. As a rule, herbs and spices are best.

Beverages

Water, water, water! It is fantastic on any diet and certainly what most cavemen would have drunk, straight from the river (you're allowed bottles or the tap). However the great news is that you can also drink pure, unsweetened fruit and vegetable juices in moderation. Tea and coffee are acceptable on the Paleo diet, plain or with almond milk but not cow's milk.

This book also offers some great ideas for refreshing drinks that are Paleo-friendly and totally delicious.

To enjoy and succeed at the Paleo diet, think quality in terms of food origin and preparation:

1. Poultry like chicken, duck, turkey and goose and their eggs should all be organic, vegetarian-raised and free of hormones.

2. Eat any seafood, particularly cold-water fish varieties like cod, haddock, mackerel and salmon to up your omega-3 intake.

3. Steam, grilling, pan-fry or bake or broil - never deep fry. Our recipes will show you the way to cook Paleo food with ease.

4. Paleo allows carrots in moderation, and unlimited onions, which were once wild.

5. Aim to choose low-glycemic fruit and vegetables, ideally organic and in season. Frozen options are allowed, if kept to a minimum, but not canned which may include excess salt, sugar and other additives.

6. Nuts, seeds and oils supply healthy fats and fill you up. Tree nut are permitted - pecans, walnuts and almonds but not peanuts (a legume). Raw is best, or if roasted, without sugar, salt or added oil.

7. Seeds and seed oils are great, full of healthy fats and antioxidants.

8. Use extra-virgin olive oil for dressings and for cooking foods at low heat, or pure olive oil or grape-seed oil for cooking at higher temperatures.

9. Don't count calories. Ever. Cavemen never did and while the calorie count may seem high, the style of eating is super-healthy and you will lose weight.

10. Aim to eat 60% protein, 35% carbs and 5% non-animal fats such as those found in nuts, seeds, avocadoes and olive oil.

11. Don't worry if you crave starchy carbs at first, this is normal. Stick with Paleo and it will pass after a few days... after all this is your *natural* diet.

12. Eat three main meals plus snacks when hungry – our 28-Day plan in Chapter 10 will get you started.

Meat, Eggs and Poultry

Beef

Buffalo

Caribou

Chicken

Duck

Eggs (fresh, no substitutes)

Elk

Emu

Goat

Goose

Grouse

Kangaroo

Offal/organ meats (tongue, gizzards, kidneys, liver, hearts)

Ostrich

Partridge

Pheasant

Pork

Quail

Rabbit

Squab

Turkey

Turtle

Venison

Wild boar

Fish

Bluefish

Cod

Eel

Flatfish

Grouper

Haddock

Halibut

Herring

Mackerel

Monkfish

Mullet

Perch

Pike

Red snapper

Rockfish

Salmon

Sardine

Scrod

Sea bass

Shark

Striped bass

Sunfish

Swordfish

Tilapia

Trout

Tuna

Turbot

Walleye

Seafood

Abalone

Brown shrimp

Clam

Cockles

Crab

Crayfish

Lobster

Mussels

Oyster

Prawns

Scallop

Shrimp

Fruit

Apple

Apricot

Avocado

Banana

Blackberry

Boysenberry

Blueberry

Carambola (star fruit)

Cherimoya (custard apple)

Cherry

Cranberry

Gooseberry

Grape

Grapefruit

Guava	**Vegetables**	Mustard greens
Kiwi	Artichoke	Onion
Lemon	Asparagus	Pak choi
Lime	Beet greens	Parsley
Lychee	Bell pepper	Pumpkin
Mango	Bok choy	Rutabaga
Melon	Broccoli	Seaweed
Nectarine	Brussels sprout	Spinach
Orange	Cabbage	Spring onion
Papaya	Cauliflower	Squash
Passion fruit	Celeriac	Swiss chard
Peach	Celery	Tomatillo
Pear	Chilli	Tomato
Pineapple	Collard greens	Turnip
Plum	Cucumber	Turnip greens
Pomegranate	Dandelion greens	Watercress
Raspberry	Eggplant/ aubergine	Zucchini/ courgette
Rhubarb	Endive	
Tangerine	Kale	
Watermelon	Kohlrabi	
	Lettuce	
	Mushroom	

Nuts, Seeds and Oils

Almond butter

Almond

Brazil nut

Cashew

Chestnut

Coconut oil

Flax seed

Hazelnut

Macadamia nut

Nut flour (almond, hazelnut etc.)

Olive oil

Pecan

Pine nut

Pistachio

Pumpkin seeds

Sesame seeds

Sunflower seeds

Sesame butter or pure, raw tahini

Walnut

Beverages

Fruit juice, pure, organic and unsweetened

Green tea

Herbal tea

Water

Miscellaneous

Carob powder

Coconut flour and milk

Dried fruit

Fresh and dried herbs

Raw, organic honey

Spices and seasonings

Foods to Avoid

Dairy

Butter

Cheese

Dairy spreads

Frozen yoghurt

Ice cream

Milk, all kinds

Yoghurt

Cereal Grains

Barley

Buckwheat

Corn (all kinds)

Millet

Oats

Rice (all kinds including rice noodles)

Rye

Sorghum

Wheat (all forms)

Legumes

All beans

Black-eyed peas

Chickpeas

Lentils

Mange tout

Miso

Peanuts and peanut butter

Peas

Snow/ sugar snap peas

Soybeans and all soy products, including tofu

Starchy Vegetables

Cassava root

Manioc

Potatoes (and all potato products)

Tapioca

Yams

Processed Meat and Snacks

Bacon (can be used in moderation, not daily)

Canned meat and fish

Chorizo

Hot dogs

Ketchup

Pickled foods

Processed meats

Salami

Sausages, fresh or smoked

Smoked, dried and salted fish and meat

Chapter 3 - The Paleo Lifestyle

Like any successful diet, it has to ultimately become a lifestyle to ensure lasting benefits. Many have quit other diets early (and therefore seen poor results) as the lifestyle is by no means enjoyable to follow. Happily, Paleo offers a great lifestyle and is easy to incorporate into daily life.

Embracing Paleo

Any lifestyle change needs you to embrace it fully to make sure you enjoy it! If you choose to go Paleo, then do it for yourself, no one else, and do it with enthusiasm. That said, you need to allow yourself a period of adjustment. Having a positive attitude will help enormously.

Be determined, particularly in the first couple of weeks. It will be tempting to 'cheat' at first by having just a little bread, or wine, or sugar... but just remember that these are really not your body's friends and you need to replace them with genuine treats, like walking by a river in the sunshine, playing with your kids, reading a book or going dancing. Then, as you start to feel better and look better, the Paleo lifestyle will become a no-brainer – your body will be telling you that this is the change it has been waiting for.

Handy Paleo Dos and Don'ts

DO choose restaurants that pride themselves on their meat, fresh seafood and fresh salad or vegetable options. Get used to sending the bread basket away without hesitation and don't take yourself off to the 'golden arches' and expect to have an easy choice.

DO drink plenty of water; it will fill you up, hydrate you, aid your digestion, support your metabolism, improve your brain function, make your skin glow and give countless other benefits to your body.

DON'T feel the need to skip meals. Eat pure Paleo, enjoy the right snacks and you won't go hungry.

DO prepare ahead by cooking up large batches of recipes, such as the curries or soups in our recipes section, and enjoying them through the week. You will be less likely to go off-Paleo if you do and you'll save time for relaxing with loved ones or spending that all important time on your own.

DON'T panic and give up if you accidentally use a non-paleo ingredient then realise afterwards. It's not the end of the world, you just have to get straight back on the Paleo bike and keep going to ensure all those great health and weight benefits.

DO make life easy by adopting or adapting our 28-day plan, and using that as a springboard to enjoy growing into the new Paleo you!

Do I, Don't I? Paleo and Alcohol

Many people who learn about the benefits of Paleo launch into it with enthusiasm, but the vast majority of new followers ask the same question:

"Sounds great. But what about alcohol?"

Most Paleo experts agree that you can drink on occasion – although there are certainly more Paleo options than others think when it comes to alcohol.

Drinking daily will undo all the good you are doing with your new lifestyle. Alcohol is toxic to the liver and some of the toxins are stored as fat. Plus it is dehydrating, full of empty calories and can cause you to crave carbs, so it is mostly best avoided by anyone who wants to lose weight.

However, in moderation it can be a sociable pleasure, especially at times of family celebration and so on, so many devote Paleo followers never say never. It is a question of preference and being sensible with your choices.

Here's the lowdown on the Paleo factor in popular drinks:

- Wine – Red wine, with its antioxidant resveratrol, is one of the most Paleo alcoholic drinks available. White wine is less so, but go organic and you will have a good, healthy drink option.

- Beer – Sorry beer lovers, but it really is not a Paleo drink! It is made from grains so, it does not suit the Paleo ethos. There are gluten-free beers, but don't be confused by them as they are still grain-based. If you are a fan, try an alternative such as...

- Cider – A natural, preservative-free, organic dry cider is another refreshing alcoholic drink that can be permitted as fairly Paleo. Delectable apple cider or pear-based versions (perry) can be enjoyed on occasion as a fruit-derived treat.

- Spirits – Once again, it depends which spirit, as some are more Paleo than others. Potato-based vodka, gin and tequila are the better options. Avoid dark spirits with caramel colourings and make sure you are not fooled into using high sugar, additive-packed mixers. A vodka, lime and soda can pass muster as Paleo, a dark rum and Coke cannot.

Finally, help your body sustain minimal lasting impact by following a few simple tips:

1. Eat only protein and veg that day, to combat fat storage.
2. Take 500 mg of vitamin C and 600 mg of Nac-Acetyl Cysteine (NAC) to help reduce the toxin liver aldehyde.

3. Take vitamin B1 or alpha lipoic acid before each drink and add 4 capsules of activated charcoal afterwards to limit alcohol's impact on your body.

If you drink, take a good break until the next time and be responsible. Enjoy!

Share the Paleo Good News!

Help yourself, and others, by spreading the word about the Paleo diet. When it works for you, let others know. Not only will you help your friends, you will also cement your own dedication to the Paleo lifestyle.

Even if friends don't change their ways, that's fine and entirely their choice. However, it is important that you tell them what you are doing and trying to achieve and why so that they don't wave cakes under your nose or try to force-feed you French fries for fun! Good friends respect each other's choices and the chances are that they will be supportive. Get creative and make it easy to pick up, where you left off. If you used to meet in bars all the time, why not invite them out to a fresh juice bar for a change? It will prove you mean what you say and they could discover new treats they enjoy too.

Chapter 4 - Losing Weight With Paleo

The Calorie Question

For years, many nutritionists have told us to avoid meat, fat and oil, avoid high-carb fruit and veg and instead go for a whole-grain high fiber diet and eat plenty of pulses, or legumes. Above all, we have been warned to keep calories low to lose weight. Paleo on the other hand promotes eating fats and proteins and cautions against sugar and starch. So who is right?

Well we know for a fact that Paleo works and is a fantastic, ultra-healthy way to lose weight. Why? Because of our Paleo programming.

Our Natural Paleo Programming

How can any diet rich in meat and animal fat plus fruit and veg help anyone shed the pounds? In truth, it is because this is what our bodies have evolved to eat over millions of years. Historically, genetically, nutritionally and psychologically, Paleo is what humans are made to eat.

Everything else has only been on our plate for a few thousand years at most. Perhaps in another million years a large bowl of pasta will be easy for us to digest, but for now it results in bloating, indigestion, a blood sugar spike and weight gain for most of us.

Paleo is the diet that made us. Our bodies, metabolism and digestive system were made for this type of eating, it really is that simple. If millions of us suddenly decided to eat loads of starch in the form of toast, cereal, sandwiches and pasta and so on every day... If we overloaded on deep-fried food and created trans-fats, added artificial ingredients and chemicals.... Furthermore if we ruined already cheap, bad quality food with loads of salt and sugar to try and create a moreish taste, and drank more alcohol than was good for us... Well then we would have a pretty overweight and unhealthy society... Aha!

Put your body back on the right track with the Paleo diet. It will thank you for all the good fats, vitamins, minerals, fiber and carbs it receives as well as the unhealthy foods it cuts out. People who follow a Paleo approach tend to be slimmer, healthier, suffer less illness and love longer than those who do not. Food for thought.

Low-Fat High-Carb Diets v Paleo

Cutting the fat in your diet and therefore the calories can work up to a point and some people lose weight quickly. The problem is that cutting out the fat can make you feel deprived and hungry.

Also, sugar-free muesli, for example, might look healthy, but what is it really doing inside our bodies? Essentially grains, which are starch are converted to sugar which mean our blood sugar levels spike then crash in a similar way to when we eat a chocolate bar. We feel tired, even depressed and crave another starch/sugar rush.

Paleo avoids this deadly seesawing. The carbs are natural, from plants, and give healthy energy, plus lots of fiber to keep you full and aid your digestive system. Protein builds muscles, which are essential for burning off fat. Your blood sugar is kept steady and you receive a whole host of beneficial nutrients such as vitamins, minerals and fatty acids. You are well nourished and therefore do not feel hungry - much better for the long-term than starving yourself or riding the sugar rollercoaster!

Eat Fat to Lose Fat

This concept is normally the one that people who are new to Paleo struggle with the most. It sounds strange, certainly, but it is medical fact. This is because we are not referring to the sort of saturated fat found in cheap, low-quality processed foods like fast-food burgers and hot dogs. This refers to Omega-3 fatty acids, which help the body and drive weight loss as they regulate insulin production.

When people develop a fat belly, is because the body cannot convert the sugar to energy, so it stores it as fat. Omega-3 fatty acids ultimately helps convert glucose into energy instead. Paleo foods are packed with omega-3 fatty acids: grass-fed meat, seafood, nuts and seeds. So, eating good fat really will help you lose fat and eating good quality protein will help build muscle, which also burns fat – which is why Paleo really works.

Now look at the following recipes packed full of nutrients, and you will see that not only will Paleo help you lose weight, but it tastes great too!

Conversion Table

Paleo is growing increasingly popular around the world so to help make your Paleo cooking easier, we have provided a measurements conversion chart. This offer United States, metric, and Imperial (U.K.) measures, (rounded off to the nearest whole number).

Dry or Weight Measurements				
		Ounces	Pounds	Metric
1/16 teaspoon	a dash			
1/8 teaspoon or less	a pinch or 6 drops		.	.5 ml
1/4 teaspoon	15 drops			1 ml
1/2 teaspoon	30 drops			2 ml
1 teaspoon	1/3 tablespoon	1/6 ounce		5 ml
3 teaspoons	1 tablespoon	1/2 ounce		14 grams
1 tablespoon	3 teaspoons	1/2 ounce		14 grams
2 tablespoons	1/8 cup	1 ounce		28 grams
4 tablespoons	1/4 cup	2 ounces		56.7 grams
5 tablespoons plus 1 teaspoon	1/3 cup	2.6 ounces		75.6 grams
8 tablespoons	1/2 cup	4 ounces	1/4 pound	113 grams
10 tablespoons plus 2 teaspoons	2/3 cup	5.2 ounces		151 grams
12 tablespoons	3/4 cup	6 ounces	.375 pound	170 grams
16 tablespoons	1 cup	8 ounces	.500 pound or 1/2 pound	225 grams
32 tablespoons	2 cups	16 ounces	1 pound	454 grams
64 tablespoons	4 cups or 1 quart	32 ounces	2 pounds	907 grams

Liquid or Volume Measurements								
	Pint	Quart	Gallon	U.S. Fluid Ounce	U.S. Tablespoon	Milliliters	Liters	U.K. Ounces
jigger or measure	-	-	-	1.5	3	45	-	-
1 cup	1/2	-	-	8	16	237	-	8.3
2 cups	1	-	-	16	32	473	0.473	19.2
4 cups	2	1	1/4	32	64	946	0.946	40

Chapter 5 - Paleo Breakfasts

Breakfast Eggs, Mushroom and Tomatoes

Prep time: 7 minutes

Cooking time: 15 minutes

A simple, filling and tasty Paleo way to start your day. Also makes a great quick dinner when you are short on time.

Serves 2

Ingredients

6 large eggs, beaten

6 cherry tomatoes

1 onion, finely chopped

1 clove garlic, crushed

225g (8 ounces) brown cap mushrooms, roughly sliced

1 teaspoon chopped thyme leaves

1 tablespoon chopped parsley, few leaves to garnish

2 teaspoons coconut oil

Method:

1. Melt 1 tsp of the coconut oil over a low-to-medium heat in a heavy saucepan.

2. Add the onion and garlic and sauté them gently for about 3-4 minutes or until translucent.

3. Tip in the mushrooms and tomatoes, stir and cook for an additional 5 minutes.

4. Add the chopped thyme and parsley plus a pinch of seasoning, then stir.

5. Remove the mixture to a bowl and keep warm.

6. Add the remaining coconut oil, turn the heat low and melt.

7. Add the eggs and season with a pinch of salt. Cook for around 3 minutes or until they just begin to set, then stir in the mushroom, onion and garlic mixture.

8. Remove from heat and stir until creamy and still just softly set.

9. Season with the remaining salt. Cook over for 3-4 minutes or just until they start to set. Add the mushroom mixture and remove from heat.

10. Garnish with the parsley leaves and eat straight away.

Prep time: 1 minute

Cooking time: 0

A super-healthy, tasty way to start any day, delivering a great burst of Omega-3 and nutrients.

Serves 2

Ingredients

6 tablespoons of black or white chia seeds

2 tablespoons organic hemp hearts

2 chopped dried organic apples

1 tbsp chopped macadamia nuts

2tbsp real cinnamon

1 tsp honey

Plus at least 3 tbsps of dairy-free coconut yoghurt or unsweetened almond milk to serve

Method:

1. Mix all the dry ingredients together in a bowl.

2. Eat your serving with the nut milk or yoghurt and drizzle over the honey.

Prep time: 10 minutes

Cooking time: 3 minutes

Protein-packed eggs and lycopene-rich tomatoes are a tasty, nutritious combination. Served on a small bed of peppery, dark green watercress, full of vitamin K, and they make satisfying and colorful breakfast or brunch.

Serves 1

Ingredients

2 organic or free-range eggs

A handful of watercress

1 medium tomato

Salt and pepper to taste

Drop of organic white vinegar

Method:

1. First, poach your eggs according to your favorite method – if you've never poached an egg before, this is a foolproof technique for poaching the old-fashioned way:

2. Put on a large saucepan of water to boil and add a pinch of salt to it.

3. Make sure your eggs are really fresh and crack each one into a ramekin or cup.

4. Add a small drop of vinegar to each egg.

5. When the water is boiling, take a hand-held balloon whisk and stir the water to create a gentle whirlpool in the water, which will help the egg white wrap around the yolk.

6. Slowly tip the eggs into the water, one after the other. Turn the heat right down to the minimum setting. Leave to cook for exactly three minutes to enjoy a soft yolk – setting a timer would be ideal.

7. While they are cooking, cut the tomato into wedges and arrange over the bed of watercress.

8. When the three minutes are up, remove the poached eggs with a slotted spoon, snipping off any straggly edges using the edge of the spoon.

9. Gently rest the eggs to drain onto kitchen paper for a few seconds, then ease them onto the bed of watercress and tomato.

Prep time: 2 minutes

Cooking time: 10 minutes

Going to Paleo does not mean you have to miss out on tasty treats like pancakes and these healthy versions are absolutely delicious. If you like, you can always double the recipe and keep a few handy in the fridge for another morning.

Makes 4 Pancakes

Ingredients

2 bananas

200ml coconut milk

4 tablespoons ground almonds

1 tablespoon raw honey

3 eggs

½ teaspoon vanilla extract

½ teaspoon nutmeg

2 tablespoons coconut oil

Method:

1. Mix all the ingredients except the coconut oil in a blender. Blend just until well mixed.

2. Melt 1 tbsp of the coconut oil in a medium skillet over a medium heat. Pour a quarter of the batter into the pan and cook until the center starts to become slightly dry. Then turn the pancake over.

3. Repeat with the rest of the batter, adding extra coconut oil if needed. Serve hot with maple syrup or warm raw honey.

Prep time: 10 minutes

Cooking time: 50 minutes

No need to miss fresh bread or toast in the mornings – it is one of life's real pleasures. This recipe makes perfect Paleo bread with a proper crust and a fluffy inner crumb. Bake the night before (or get up early!) and enjoy it topped with mashed banana or raspberries, or just some thin slices of cold roast meat, or a poached egg, or just some coconut oil spread over it.

Ingredients:

60g coconut flour, sifted

30g psyllium husk powder

6 eggs separated into yolks and whites

4 tbsp coconut oil, melted

120ml dairy-free coconut yoghurt

2 tsp apple cider vinegar

1 ½ tsp baking soda

¼ tsp salt

Method:

1. Preheat oven to 350°F – don't skip this step as it will ensures the bread rises well.

2. Line an approximately 8.5 × 4.5 inch loaf pan with parchment paper.

3. Whip the egg whites until they form soft, foamy peaks.

4. Blend the coconut oil and yoghurt into the egg yolks until smooth and creamy.

5. Sift the coconut flour, psyllium husk powder, baking soda and salt into the egg yolk and yoghurt mixture then blend again. It will be thick, but that's fine. Add the apple cider vinegar and give it a final blending so there are no lumps.

6. Gently fold in the egg whites to make a smooth batter but do not beat out all the air.

7. Pour the bread mixture into the loaf pan, smoothing off the top.

8. Bake the loaf for around 50 minutes, leaving it to rest in the pan for 10 minutes after you remove it from the oven, then enjoy!

Prep time: 1 minute

Cooking time: 0

Smoothies are great for when you are in a hurry. This one is fast to make and tastes really creamy and fresh.

Serves 2

Ingredients

2 bananas

225ml (8 fluid ounces) unflavoured, unsweetened almond milk

4 tablespoons water

2 tablespoons raw honey

8 ice cubes

Method:

1. Place all of the ingredients, except for the ice cubes, into a blender. Blend on high until smooth.

2. Add the ice cubes and blend again until thick and creamy.

Prep time: 1 minute

Cooking time: 0

If you haven't tried one before, you should discover the healthy delights of drinking a green smoothie for breakfast. It is a great way of getting some greens in and each drink is bursting with nutrients, plus it only takes seconds to prepare.

Serves 2

Ingredients

1 cup fresh spinach leaves

1 cup fresh watercress

1 pint unsweetened apricot nectar

1 banana

Method:

Place all ingredients in a blender and blend on high for 1 minute or slightly longer until very smooth. Drink immediately.

⬛

Coconut and Macadamia Pancakes

Prep time: 2 minutes

Cooking time: 10 minutes

These pancakes are full of nuts with great, healthy fats and will keep your motor running through the most hectic of mornings. Make extra and keep them in the fridge for up to four days.

Makes 4 – 6 Pancakes

2 tablespoons coconut flour

1 pint coconut milk

4 large eggs

½ pint water

½ pint of chopped macadamia nuts

1 teaspoon cinnamon

3 teaspoons coconut oil

Method:

1. Place the coconut flour, coconut milk, eggs, water and cinnamon in a blender and blend on low speed until smooth. Pour into a measuring jug.

2. Stir in the macadamia nuts.

3. Heat one teaspoon of the coconut oil in a large heavy skillet over medium-high heat. Pour in enough batter to make a four-inch pancake. Cook until the center is almost dry (about three minutes) then turn. Cook for one more minute then place on a covered plate to keep warm.

4. Repeat with the remaining batter. Serve hot with maple syrup or raw honey.

Prep time: 10 minutes

Cooking time: 10 minutes

This makes a fun, filling, healthy breakfast that is packed with exciting flavors. Great for when you want a meal that will keep you going for hours. Paleo mornings have never tasted so amazing!

Makes 2 Burritos

Ingredients

4 eggs, whites and yolks separated

1/2 onion, finely chopped

1 to 2 tomatoes, finely chopped

1/4 cup canned diced green chilies

1 red pepper, cut into strips

1/4 cup finely chopped cilantro (coriander)

1/2 cup cooked meat (try sliced steak, ground beef, or shredded chicken)

1 avocado, cut into wedges or small chunks

2 tsps coconut oil

For the Paleo Salsa (optional)

6 roma tomatoes, coarsely chopped

1/2 red onion, coarsely chopped

1 lime, juiced

1/2 bunch cilantro (coriander), chopped

1 jalapeno pepper, chopped

1 habanero pepper, chopped

1 clove garlic, chopped

A pinch of black pepper

Salsa Method:

Combine tomatoes, onion, lime juice, cilantro, jalapeno pepper, habanero pepper, garlic, and black pepper in a food processor. Pulse several times until blended to your preference.

Burrito Method:

1. Whisk the egg whites while warming half the coconut oil in a 10-inch skillet.

2. Pour half of the egg whites in the pan, swirling the pan around so the whites spread thinly and evenly.

3. After about 30 seconds, put a lid on the pan and cook 1 minute more.

4. Use a rubber spatula to ease the egg white "tortilla" onto a plate. Repeat with the remaining egg whites.

5. Now sauté the onions with oil for one minute then add tomato, green chilies, red pepper, cilantro, and meat.

6. Whisk the egg yolks and pour into the pan, mixing everything together into a scramble.

7. Add avocado right at the end, then spoon half of filling onto each egg white 'tortilla'. Roll the egg whites up into burritos and serve with the Paleo salsa if you fancy.

Chapter 6 – Paleo Lunches

Spinach and Bacon Salad

Prep time: 2 minutes

Cooking time: 15 minutes

Remember how powerful Popeye was? Time to top up your iron with this tasty spinach lunch. Bacon is not a meat to eat daily, but many devoted Paleo followers enjoy a little from time to time.

Serves 2

Ingredients:

4 large eggs

8 rashers uncured, unsmoked bacon or pancetta

300g (11 ounces) fresh spinach

1 small red onion, sliced

6 tablespoons olive oil

3 tablespoons lemon juice

2 cloves garlic, crushed

¼ teaspoon salt

¼ teaspoon freshly ground black pepper

Method:

1. Place the eggs in a saucepan with cold water and bring the water to the boil; cover, remove from heat, and let eggs stand for 10 to 12 minutes.

2. Drain and place in a cold bowl of water to cool. Once the eggs have cooled, peel and chop them into wedges and set aside.

3. Meanwhile, heat a large heavy skillet over medium high heat and cook the bacon until evenly browned, turning once. Drain on kitchen towels then chop and set aside.

4. In a medium bowl, mix together the eggs, bacon, spinach and onion.

5. In a separate bowl, whisk together the oil, lemon juice, garlic, salt and pepper. Pour over the salad and toss well to coat.

?

Prep time: 5 minutes

Cooking time: 0 (best chilled for 1 hour)

This is a light but satisfying lunch that will take you straight to the summery hills of Tuscany… Easy to make and perfect for when you have guests.

Serves 2

Ingredients

1 pound cooked chicken breast, diced

1 bulb fennel, trimmed of the fronds and sliced

2 blood oranges, peeled and sliced

2 x 100g bags wild rocket – chopped

2 tablespoons olive oil

2 tablespoons red wine vinegar

1 teaspoon poppy seeds

Salt and pepper to taste

Method:

1. Combine the cooked chicken, oranges and fennel in a generous bowl.

2. In a small jug, whisk together the olive oil, red wine vinegar, poppy seeds, salt and pepper and pour over the salad.

3. Toss well to coat every ingredient and refrigerate for at least one hour.

4. Remove the chicken mixture from the fridge and add the rocket. Toss again and serve cold.

Chicken, Leek and Cauliflower Soup

Prep time: 10 minutes

Cooking time: 55 minutes

This is a delicious soup, based on the British favorite, Cock-a-Leekie. This flavor-laden version really hits the spot and you can make large batches and freeze them, or take it to the office in a flask.

Ingredients

300g chicken thighs, bone and skin removed, chopped

300g cauliflower, chopped into small florets

2 large leeks, trimmed and washed

1.2 litres chicken stock

1 bouquet of Garni

8 prunes, chopped

½ teaspoon salt

¼ teaspoon freshly ground black pepper

2 tablespoons chopped fresh parsley to garnish

1 tablespoon light olive oil

Method:

1. In a large non-stick saucepan, heat the oil over a medium-high heat. Add the chicken to the pan and sauté for 5 minutes, stirring often until evenly browned all over. Remove from the pan and drain on kitchen paper.

2. Trim the coarse dark green ends of the leeks and set aside. Slice the remaining white parts and add them to the pan. Fry for 5 minutes or until soft, stirring frequently.

3. Add the stock and bouquet of Garni to the pan and add the chicken once more. Season with salt and pepper, then bring to the boil.

4. Reduce the heat to low, cover and simmer for 30 minutes or until tender.

5. Finely slice the green parts of the leeks, then add them to the pan, along with the cauliflower and prunes. Cover and simmer for 10 more minutes.

6. Remove the bouquet of Garni, ladle the soup into bowls and garnish with the fresh chopped parsley.

Haddock and Sweet Potato Chowder

Prep time: 7 minutes

Cooking time: 1 hr 45

This delicious fish goes brilliantly well with sweet potato, turning this chowder into a fabulous, warming dish. Soups are so convenient, so make plenty and it will last you for lunches or light suppers.

Serves 4

Ingredients

200g unsmoked haddock, with skin

500ml coconut milk

500ml homemade or organic seafood stock

1 stalk celery, sliced thinly

1 large carrot, sliced thinly

1 leek, sliced

1 large sweet potato, peeled and diced

2 sprigs thyme

¼ teaspoon freshly ground black pepper

¼ teaspoon nutmeg

1 teaspoon coconut oil

1 onion, finely chopped

1 clove garlic, finely chopped

Method:

1. Place a large saucepan over medium-high heat and place the fish into the bottom.

2. Add the coconut milk, seafood stock, thyme and pepper. Bring to the boil, then remove from the heat and let it rest for one hour.

3. Afterwards, remove the fish from the liquid, remove the skin and any small bones and tear into bite-sized (no smaller) pieces, then set aside.

4. Remove the thyme sprigs from the cooking liquid and discard them.

5. Heat the coconut oil in another large pan. Add the onions, leek, garlic, celery and carrots and gently sauté until just soft and sweet, approximately 10 minutes.

6. Add the sautéed vegetables to the cooking liquid, and add the sweet potato.

7. Bring to the boil and then reduce heat to low and simmer for about half an hour.

8. Use a hand blender and pulse for just few seconds until thicker but still chunky.

9. Add the fish back into the chowder and stir to heat everything through. Ladle into deep bowls and serve hot.

Mushroom, Courgette and Pancetta Frittata

Prep time: 5 minutes

Cooking time: 17 minutes

Serves 2 - 4

Ingredients:

6 large eggs

150g unsmoked pancetta, diced.

150g button mushrooms chopped

300g leeks, shredded

2 tablespoons coconut oil, as required

Pinch of salt and pepper

Method:

1. Fry the pancetta for 5 minutes in a medium-sized skillet. Let it crisp then remove and set aside on kitchen paper, leaving the rendered fat in the pan.

2. Fry the mushrooms in the pancetta fat until they are golden, adding a little coconut oil if necessary,. Set aside when done.

3. Add the leeks to the pan. If dry add some more oil, cover and cook over a low heat until soft and sweet, but not browned.

4. Break all the eggs into a bowl, whisk well and season with the salt and pepper. Return the pancetta and mushrooms to the pan with the leeks, then pour over the beaten egg.

5. Leave the frittata to cook over a low heat, until the bottom is golden and the edges are beginning to set.

6. In the meantime, warm an overhead grill, place the pan under the heat and leave for a few minutes until the egg has set lightly, but still has a gentle wobble.

7. Serve hot with some Paleo bread, or with a fresh green salad.

Prep time: 10 minutes

Cooking time: 25-30 minutes

Enjoy this on a lazy Saturday for brunch – the lovely roasted veg goes beautifully with eggs for a warm, tasty, healthy hit of protein, vitamins, good fats and fiber.

Serves 4

Ingredients

½ red pepper, sliced

½ green pepper, sliced

1 medium aubergine, cut into bite sized pieces

1 medium fennel bulb, sliced

1 medium onion, sliced

4 large eggs

1 garlic clove, chopped

2 tablespoons fresh rosemary

2 tablespoons fresh parsley

3 tablespoons olive oil

Method:

1. Preheat the oven to 200 C / Gas 6.

2. Lay the vegetables in a baking pan and sprinkle with the rosemary and parsley. Drizzle over the olive oil and toss until well-coated.

3. Roast the vegetables in the oven for about 20 minutes or until the aubergine is tender.

4. Remove the vegetables and make four small depressions in them. Crack one egg into each depression and return to the oven.

5. Cook for another 5-10 minutes, depending on how you like your eggs. Remove from the oven, cut into four portions with one egg each and serve immediately.

Prep time: 8 minutes

Cooking time: 12 minutes

This classic French recipe sounds strange but it really is delicious, with the sharp sweetness of the berries contrasting with the earthy, savory chicken livers. Try it and you will be surprised by how moreish it is.

Serves 4

Ingredients

400 g (14 oz) chicken livers

125 g (4½ oz) raspberries

3 tablespoons raspberry vinegar

150 g (5½ oz) mixed baby lettuce leaves

100 g (3½ oz) baby spinach leaves

4 tablespoons chopped fresh parsley

4 tablespoons snipped fresh chives

100 g (3½ oz) shallots, finely chopped

1 large garlic clove, crushed

3 tablespoons extra virgin olive oil, divided

Salt and pepper to taste

Method:

1. Trim the chicken livers, removing any membrane tissue, and cutting bigger pieces in half. Pat the livers dry with some kitchen paper, then set aside.

2. Mix together the lettuce, spinach, parsley and chives and set aside as well.

3. Heat 2 tablespoons of the olive oil in a skillet. Add the shallots and garlic and cook for about 2 minutes over a medium heat or until softened, stirring frequently.

4. Increase the heat to medium-high and add the remaining tablespoon of olive oil to the pan. Add the chicken livers and cook, stirring frequently, for about 5 minutes or until they are cooked - there should be just a hint of pink in the centre.

5. Add the raspberry vinegar to the pan and stir, scraping up any browned bits from the bottom. Season the mixture with the salt and pepper to taste.

6. Remove from heat and allow it to cool until very warm, but no longer hot. Pour the liver mixture over the salad, top with the berries and serve immediately.

[?]

Prep time: 5 minutes

Cooking time: 10 minutes

This is a really tasty carrot soup with a touch of spice to keep it lively. Makes a great weekday lunch.

Serves 2

Ingredients

5 large carrots, chopped

1 small onion, peeled and chopped

1 green apple, chopped

½ ounce fresh ginger, chopped

2 tablespoons coconut oil

⅓ cup orange juice

1 can coconut milk

2 cups chicken stock or water

⅛ teaspoon cayenne pepper (optional)

Garnish with fresh lime

Method:

1. Heat the coconut oil in a large saucepan.

2. Sauté the onion, carrot, and apple in coconut oil until tender.

3. Add the ginger to the saucepan, followed by the orange juice, coconut milk and stock.

4. Heat the mixture in the pan, stirring in cayenne pepper.

5. Garnish with fresh lime and serve.

Prep time: 5 minutes

Cooking time: 45 minutes

These are like Scotch eggs – but totally Paleo! The fresh pork mince, instead of processed sausage, makes all the difference and they taste outstanding.

Ingredients:

4 large eggs

500g fresh pork mince

½ teaspoon salt

½ teaspoon freshly ground black pepper

½ cup chopped fresh parsley

½ teaspoon dried rosemary

1 tablespoon coconut oil

Paleo Coating

1 cup almond flour

1/2 teaspoon sea salt

1/2 teaspoon black pepper

1/2 teaspoon garlic powder

1/2 teaspoon dried parsley

1/4 teaspoon onion powder

1/4 teaspoon dried oregano

Coating Method:

Mix all ingredients together in a small bowl with a mini-whisk or fork until thoroughly combined. Reserve.

Porky Eggs Method:

1. Place the eggs in a saucepan of water and bring to the boil over high heat. Cover, remove from heat and allow them to rest for 15 minutes. Then place in a bowl of cold water to cool.

2. In a large mixing bowl, combine the pork mince, salt, pepper, parsley and rosemary and mix well.

3. Divide the mince into four patties about 1/2 inch thick.

4. Peel the eggs and place one egg in the center of each patty. Use your hands to mold the patty around the egg, taking care that there are no gaps or tears.

5. Roll the eggs in the Paleo coating.

6. Preheat the oven to 180°C and heat the coconut oil in a large skillet.

7. Brown the eggs on all sides for about 10 minutes total, then place into a baking dish and bake for another 15 minutes. Serve hot or cold.

?

Prep time: 5 minutes

Cooking time: 0 (best chilled overnight)

This lovely summer lunch makes a tasty twist on the normal salad as it is lightly curried and features some pineapple for a delicious contrast.

Ingredients

1 (400g) tin tuna in spring water, drained and flaked

(220g) tin unsweetened pineapple chunks, drained

2 ripe avocadoes, stoned and halved

60g cashews, roughly chopped

2 tablespoons olive oil mayonnaise

½ tablespoon curry powder

1 teaspoon raw honey

½ teaspoon salt

¼ teaspoon freshly ground black pepper

Method:

1. In a medium mixing bowl, combine the tuna, mayonnaise, curry powder, honey, salt and pepper and stir until well-combined.

2. Stir in the pineapple chunks and cashews, cover and refrigerate overnight.

3. To serve, spoon 1/4 of the filling into each avocado half and enjoy.

Chapter 7 – Paleo Dinners

Paleo Pot Roast

Prep time: 7 minutes

Cooking time: 35 minutes

This is a wonderfully simple beef dish, but it is packed with flavor. Enjoy it just as it is or with a refreshing green side salad.

Ingredients

1 tablespoon olive oil

1 (2kg) silverside roasting joint

1 onion, chopped

4 large carrots, peeled and cut into chunks

2 cloves garlic, minced

2 bay leaves

½ teaspoon salt, divided

½ teaspoon freshly ground black pepper, divided

Method:

1. Preheat oven to 160 C / Gas 3.

2. Heat a casserole dish on the hob over medium heat. Add the olive oil, and sear the beef joint for 4 minutes on each side until well-browned. Remove the joint from dish.

3. Place the onions, carrots, garlic, and bay leaf in the bottom of the dish, place the meat on top, seasoning all with the salt and pepper.

4. Roast in the oven for 30 minutes. Reduce heat to 150 C / Gas mark 2, and cook for an additional 1 1/2 hours.

5. Remove the joint to a platter and allow it to rest for 15 minutes.

6. To serve, slice the meat diagonally and place on each plate, surround with the carrots and topped with the onions and pan juices.

Lemon and Garlic Turkey

Prep time: 5 minutes

Cooking time: 20 minutes

Turkey is not just for the holiday season – you can enjoy it all year round thanks to this easy, effective dish. Serve hot over salad leaves – tastes great the next day too.

Ingredients

4 skinless, boneless turkey breast fillets

4 cloves crushed garlic

Juice and zest of half a large lemon

1 teaspoon chopped fresh parsley

1 teaspoon chopped fresh cilantro (coriander)

½ teaspoon salt

¼ teaspoon freshly ground black pepper

1 teaspoon raw honey

Half of one large lemon, thinly sliced

2 tablespoons olive oil

Method:

1. Heat the oil in a large frying pan over medium heat and cut the turkey breast into bite-sized pieces.

2. Fry the turkey pieces in the hot oil until browned on all sides, about 7-8 minutes.

3. Add the garlic, lemon zest and lemon juice, coriander, salt and pepper and continue to cook until the turkey is no longer pink in the middle, about 8-10 minutes.

4. Remove from heat and spoon onto plates. Sprinkle with fresh parsley and garnish with slices of the lemon. Makes 4 servings.

Prep time: 5 minutes

Cooking time: 50 minutes

Family and friends will love this mild, easy curry, which is great for informal Paleo entertaining.

Ingredients

3 chicken breasts, cut into chunks

1 tablespoon of coconut oil

1 cup of coconut cream

1 cup chicken stock

2 cups diced carrots

1 cup chopped celery

2 tomatoes, diced

1½ tablespoons good quality curry powder

1 tablespoon grated ginger

¼ cup cilantro, roughly chopped

6 cloves garlic, minced

Salt to taste

Method:

1. Sauté the chicken pieces in the coconut oil in a saucepan.

2. When the chicken is sealed and has turned white on the outside, add the stock and coconut cream, mixing well.

3. Add in the carrots, celery, and tomatoes.

4. Add in the ginger and curry powder.

5. Cover and simmer for 40 minutes (stirring occasionally).

6. Add in the minced garlic and cilantro and salt to taste.

7. Simmer for another 5 minutes and serve.

Baked Trout with Lemon and Herbs

Prep time: 7 minutes

Cooking time: 25 minutes

Fresh fish is always a real treat and your Paleo palate is sure to appreciate this clean-tasting, herby dish.

Serves 2

Ingredients

2 small whole trout

2 cloves garlic, chopped

1 lemon, sliced

2 large tomatoes, sliced into rounds

4 shallots, sliced

2 sprigs fresh basil

2 sprigs fresh rosemary

2 sprigs fresh parsley

1 tbsp olive oil

Salt and ground black pepper

Method:

1. Preheat the oven to 180°C.

2. Line the cavity of each fish with half of the garlic and lemon, then tuck in the sprigs of thyme and basil. Season the tops of the fish with salt and pepper.

3. Arrange the slices of shallots and tomato in an ovenproof dish big enough to lie the fish on top. Drizzle with the olive oil.

4. Place in the oven to bake for 25 minutes or until the fish is just done. Serve hot, garnished with fresh parsley.

Cauliflower Crust Cottage Pie

Prep time: 5 minutes

Cooking time: 40 minutes

This pie is superb, like a Paleo version of a beefy cottage pie. The cauliflower crust replaces the traditional potato, for a deliciously satisfying dish.

For the topping

1 large head cauliflower, cut into florets

2 tbsp coconut oil, melted

1 tsp mustard

2 tsps olive oil

Salt and freshly ground black pepper, to taste

Fresh parsley, to garnish

For the bottom

1 lb. lean ground beef

1/2 large onion, diced

3 carrots, diced

2 celery stalks, diced

2 tbsp tomato paste

1 cup chicken broth

1 tsp dry mustard

1/4 tsp cinnamon

1/8 tsp ground cloves

1 tbsp coconut oil

Salt and freshly ground black pepper, to taste

Method:

1. Steam the cauliflower for 14 minutes until tender – you can use a metal colander above a pot of boiling water if you don't have a steamer.

2. Place the steamed cauliflower in a large pot with the 2 tbsp of coconut oil, mustard and seasoning. Blend with a hand blender until smooth and set aside.

3. Meanwhile, heat the coconut oil in a large skillet over medium heat. Add the onion, celery, and carrots and sauté for 5 minutes. Add in the ground beef and cook until browned.

4. Stir in the tomato paste, chicken broth, and remaining spices then season to taste.

5. Simmer until most of the liquid has evaporated, about 7 or 8 minutes.

6. Share the beef mixture evenly between four ramekins and spread the pureed cauliflower on top

7. Use a fork to fluff up the cauliflower and drizzle the pie tops with olive oil.

8. Place under the grill for up to 7 minutes until the top turns golden, then sprinkle with fresh parsley and serve.

Turkey Quinoa Bolognese

Prep time: 10 minutes

Cooking time: 12 minutes

Everyone loves bolognese and this great turkey version makes a welcome change, especially when served with warm quinoa instead of pasta in a tasty Paleo twist.

Serves 4

2 cups lean turkey mince

2 cups cooked quinoa, kept warm

2 x 400g cans chopped tomatoes

2 large carrots, diced

1 clove of garlic

A pinch of dried mixed herbs

2 tsp olive oil for preparation

Green salad leaves

Method:

1. Heat the oil in a large skillet, on a medium-high heat.

2. Add the turkey mince and fry slowly, taking care to break up any large lumps with a wooden spoon.

3. Add the dried carrot and stir for a 1 or 2 minutes.

4. When the turkey is just sealed but not turning brown, add the chopped tomatoes to the pan.

5. Crush the garlic and add it to the turkey sauce, along with the herbs. Leave to simmer gently for 5 minutes or until the sauce begins to thicken.

6. Serve the sauce on a small bed of warm quinoa, with some green salad leaves on the side.

Prep time: 5 minutes

Cooking time: 15 minutes

The wild-caught snapper in this delicious dish is a real high-protein treat. The mustard gives it a great kick too – enjoy with a green salad.

Serves 4

4 x 6oz yellowtail snapper fillets, skin on

2 cups chopped seeded plum tomato

1 tbsp Dijon mustard

3 garlic cloves, minced

1 1/2 tbsp chopped fresh flat-leaf parsley

1 1/2 tbsp minced fresh chives

1 tbsp minced fresh tarragon

1 1/2 tbsp olive oil

1 tbsp coconut oil

A large pinch of freshly ground black pepper, divided

A pinch of salt

Method:

1. Heat the olive oil in a medium skillet over medium-high heat.

2. Add the tomato to pan and cook for 5 minutes, stirring frequently.

3. Stir in the capers, Dijon mustard and minced garlic, allow to simmer for 3 minutes or until slightly thickened, stirring occasionally.

4. Remove from heat and stir in the parsley, chives, tarragon, salt and black pepper. Cover to keep warm.

5. Heat the coconut oil in a large nonstick skillet over medium-high heat.

6. Season the snapper lightly and add it to the pan, skin side down.

7. Cook for 3 minutes or until skin is browned, then turn the fish over; cook for a further 3 minutes or until it is as done as you like. Serve the fish with the sauce.

Butternut Chicken

Prep time: 8 minutes

Cooking time: 50 minutes

Butternut squash boasts a lot of antioxidants and vitamins. Gem squash is also packed with carotene, to help ward off a wide range of diseases including heart disease. Enjoy this hearty simply dinner, which tastes great and is so easy to make.

Ingredients

4 skinless chicken breasts

2 butternut squashes, halved and de-seeded

2 gem squashes halved and de-seeded

4 medium tomatoes, halved

2 tbsp olive oil

A pinch of cinnamon

A large handful of torn fresh cilantro (coriander)

Method:

1. Preheat the oven to 350°F.

2. Sprinkle the butternut squashes with a little cinnamon. Place them, along with the gem squashes, on baking trays and drizzle all with half the oil. Leave them in the oven to roast.

3. After 20 minutes drizzle the chicken breasts with the remaining oil and place on another baking tray, along with the tomatoes, for at least 25 minutes.

4. When the chicken is done, remove everything from the oven. Take chunky scoops of butternut and gem squash with a spoon, pile them on each plate with the tomatoes and chicken and scatter plenty of fresh coriander over the dishes, then serve.

Prep time: 10 minutes

Cooking time: 1 hr 20 minutes

This rich, filling pie uses mashed sweet potatoes for the gorgeous golden crust. So tempting, that it is sure to become a family favorite, so make plenty!

Serves 4

Ingredients

200 g (7 oz) small button onions, peeled

500 g (1 lb 2 oz) boneless haunch or shoulder of venison shoulder, diced

1 kg (2lbs) sweet potatoes, peeled and cubed

150 g (5½ oz) baby button mushrooms

3 celery stalks, thickly sliced

1 tablespoon fresh thyme

1 tablespoon fresh rosemary

450 ml (15 floz) good beef stock

1½ teaspoons arrowroot powder

2 tablespoons extra virgin olive oil

½ teaspoon salt

½ teaspoon freshly ground black pepper

1 tablespoon wholegrain mustard

Grated zest and juice of 1 orange

Method:

1. Preheat the oven to 190°C.

2. Heat the oil in a large saucepan over medium heat and add the onions. Cook for about 5 minutes, stirring occasionally, until the onions are just lightly browned then set aside.

3. Add the venison to the pan and sauté for 2–3 minutes or until well browned.

4. Add the onions, mushrooms, sliced celery, rosemary and thyme. Pour the stock over all, and scrape the sticky scraps from the bottom of the pan to add flavor.

5. Bring to the boil and then reduce the heat to low. Cover and simmer for 45 minutes or until the meat is tender.

6. Meanwhile, boil the sweet potatoes for 15 minutes until tender. Drain, add the mustard, orange zest, orange juice, salt and pepper and mash with a fork or hand blender.

7. Blend the arrowroot powder with 2 tablespoons cold of water and whisk into the venison mixture and cook, stirring constantly, until slightly thickened.

8. Spoon the venison mixture into small pie dishes and smooth the sweet potato mash.

9. Bake for 20 minutes then serve nice and hot.

Prep time: 5 minutes

Cooking time: 35 minutes

Pork tenderloin is very tasty, especially when well-seasoned. The meat goes perfectly with some freshly steamed kale.

Serves 4

1 1/4 pounds pork tenderloin

1 tsp garlic powder

1 tsp dried oregano

1 tsp ground cumin

1 tsp ground coriander

1 tsp dried thyme

1 tbsp olive oil

1 tsp minced garlic

A pinch of salt

To serve:

12 large kale leaves, chopped

Method:

1. Preheat the oven to 450 degrees F.

2. In a separate bowl mix the dry ingredients such as garlic powder, oregano, cumin, coriander, thyme and salt. Stir the mixture with a fork until all the ingredients are well combined and they form a seasoning.

3. Put a pan of water on another ring and bring it to the boil.

4. Sprinkle the seasoning rub over the tenderloin with a dry hand. Then rub the pork with the seasoning over both sides of the meat, pressing gently so the seasoning sticks well to the surface of the tenderloin.

5. In a large skillet over medium-high heat, add the olive oil and heat.

6. Add the minced garlic and sauté, stirring, for 1 minute.

7. Put the tenderloin into the pan and brown it to seal in the juices for about 10 minutes, searing each side and carefully using tongs to turn the meat.

8. Next, transfer the meat to a roasting pan and bake for 20 minutes.

9. While the pork is cooking, steam the kale for 4 minutes.

10. When the tenderloin is ready, slice it into thick medallions and serve with the tender kale.

Chapter 8 – Paleo Beverages

Sunset Fizz

This is a bright orange-red fizz that is great as a sparkling treat or for serving to guests. You can use a pure mineral water and you may or may not wish to use Stevia as some Paleo fans are undecided about this plant-based sweetener.

Ingredients

3 blood oranges, juiced

1 ruby or pink grapefruit, juices

2 cups chilled sparkling mineral water

10 drops Valencia orange stevia drops (optional)

Method:

1. Combine all the ingredients, stir and serve over ice straight away.

Summer Sparkle

Totally refreshing, this unusual drink is a great Paleo party cooler.

Ingredients

8oz rhubarb, chopped

2 tbsp still water

1 cup sparkling water

6 oz raspberries

2 limes, juiced

½ tsp Stevia (optional)

Lime wedges to serve

Method:

1. Puree the rhubarb and the still water in a blender or food processor for about one minute.

2. Strain out the juice from the pulp and reserve.

3. In a bowl, mash the raspberries with a fork. If you want a smooth drink sieve the fruit again, or put in the mashed berries for a more full-bodied drink.

4. Mix the raspberry fruit juice with the rhubarb juice and add the lime juice. Stir and top up with sparkling water.

5. Serve over crushed ice, add a slice of lime and enjoy very cold.

This is another great cooler for serving to guests, whether they are Paleo followers or not. The ginger adds a great kick so no one misses the alcohol at all in this interesting, flavourful, sophisticated drink.

Ingredients:

4 large ripe peaches

1 tbsp lime juice

2 tsp grated ginger

2 tbsp honey (optional, to taste)

3 - 5 cups chilled sparkling mineral water

Method:

1. De-stone the peaches and puree them in a blender.

2. Add the add lime juice, ginger, and honey to the peach puree. Blend again briefly to mix.

3. Pour the puree mixture into a tall jug and slowly add the sparkling water.

4. Serve in glasses garnished with lime or peach slices.

Banapple Dream Smoothie

This creamy, indulgent drink makes the perfect sweet, smooth alternative to a milkshake.

Ingredients

1 cup almond milk or coconut milk

½ cup water

1 cup chopped red apples

1 banana

1 tsp cinnamon powder

1 tsp vanilla extract

1 tbsp almonds

A few ice cubes

Method:

1. Blend all the ingredients until smooth and creamy, then serve cold.

The perfect alternative to a sugary fizzy drink on a hot summers day.

Ingredients

Juice of 10 lemons

8 cups water

1 cup raw honey

1 pint strawberries, washed and stems removed

Method:

1. Squeeze the lemon juice and de-stem the strawberries.

2. Place the strawberries in a food processor and blend until smooth.

3. In a saucepan over a medium-high heat, combine all the lemon juice, 1 cup of water, the raw honey and the strawberries.

4. Bring the mixture just to the boil, stirring well.

5. Pour the remaining 7 cups of water into a jug, pour in the lemon-strawberry mixture and stir.

6. Taste to test the balance - you can add more lemon juice or honey to taste at this stage.

7. Refrigerate for a few hours until thoroughly chilled and serve over ice.

Chapter 9 – Paleo Snack Ideas

A piece of fruit or a carrot stick is fabulous when you are feeling peckish, but here are some more creative Paleo snack ideas:

- Stuff dates with walnuts for a sweet treat.

- Halve hard-boiled eggs, drizzle with a little olive oil and season with salt and paprika for a tasty protein hit.

- A berry salad gives a refreshing a boost or light pudding – just mix raspberries, strawberries, blackberries, blueberries and redcurrants. Drizzle with a little honey and garnish with torn mint.

- Make kale crisps by tearing the leaves into pieces, coating them with oil, salt, pepper and paprika and baking for 30 minutes, turning once.

- Create homemade banana chips. Fry sliced green bananas in coconut oil until crisp, drain and dust with salt.

- Mash cold leftover salmon or trout with avocado and spread on Paleo toast.

- Roast 5 spears of asparagus, drizzled with olive oil in a 350°F oven for a few minutes until just tender. Sprinkle with a little salt and eat hot.

- Try crunching 2/3 of a tablespoon of mixed seeds that includes pumpkin, sesame, sunflower seeds and more for some delicious healthy fats. Toast them in a hot oven for a few minutes for more flavor.

- Make some cinnamon apple chips. Preheat the oven to 200 F. Thinly slice two apples crosswise about 1/8-inch (2 mm) thick with a mandolin or sharp knife. Arrange apple slices in a single layer on baking sheets. Sprinkle 1 teaspoon of cinnamon over the apple slices. Bake for 2 hours or until apples are dry and crisp, then eat.

Chapter 10 – Your 28-Day Starter Plan

Try using these four weeks of meal suggestions to help you kick off your Paleo lifestyle.

MONDAY	TUESDAY	WEDNESDAY	THURSDAY	FRIDAY	SATURDAY	SUNDAY
Eggs, Mushroom Tomato Hawaiian Tuna Avocadoes Paleo Pot Roast	Banana and Almond Pancakes Spinach and Bacon Salad Turkey Quinoa	Paleo Loaf Chicken, Leek Soup Baked Trout	Nutty Chia Chicken Liver and Raspberry Spiced Pork	Green Smoothie Mushroom, Pancetta Frittata Lemon and Garlic Turkey	Eggs Tricolore Italian Chicken Salad Cauliflower Cottage Pie	Coconut and Macadamia Pancakes Paleo Porky Eggs Chicken Coconut Curry
Banana Smoothie Mediterranean Veg with Eggs Butternut Chicken	Eggs, Mushroom Tomato Haddock Chowder Venison and Mushroom Pie	Nutty Chia Italian Chicken Salad Roast Snapper	Green Smoothie Hawaiian Tuna Avocadoes Pot Roast	Paleo Loaf Spinach and Bacon Salad Turkey Quinoa	Caveman Burritos Chicken, Leek Soup Spiced Pork	Banana Pancakes Mushroom, Pancetta Frittata Cauliflower Cottage Pie
Eggs Tricolore Chicken Liver and Raspberry Baked Trout	Green Smoothie Mediterranean Veg with Eggs Butternut Chicken	Banana Pancakes Haddock Chowder Paleo Pot Roast	Banana Smoothie Italian Chicken Salad Cauliflower Cottage Pie	Eggs, Mushroom, Tomato Spinach and Bacon Salad Lemon and Garlic Turkey	Nutty Chia Hawaiian Tuna Avocadoes Chicken Coconut Curry	Caveman Burritos Carrot Soup Roast Snapper
Banana Pancakes Chicken, Leek Soup Spiced Pork with Greens	Eggs, Mushroom Tomatoes Italian Chicken Salad Venison and Mushroom Pie	Banana Smoothie Paleo Porky Eggs Turkey Quinoa	Nutty Chia Mushroom, Pancetta Frittata Butternut Chicken	Green Smoothie Chicken Liver and Raspberry Baked Trout	Paleo Loaf Haddock Chowder Paleo Pot Roast	Eggs Tricolore Spinach and Bacon Salad Cauliflower Cottage Pie

Loving Your Paleo Life...

Congratulations! Now you have all the tools you need to embark on your Paleo adventure. The healthiest journey you have ever taken can begin with just a few weeks, but with so many other Paleo followers, you could feel so great that you make it last a lifetime.

Whatever you choose, however you approach your own unique Paleo experience, embrace it fully. Tell your friends and colleagues, try the recipes and create your own, exchange your bad habits for good ones and you will soon notice a difference.

Take up some exercise to support your body and promote weight loss. It is entirely authentic as Paleolithic man walked miles in search of prey, so even if you sit at a laptop all day, as so many of us do, make sure you get out and enjoy the fresh air – your body and mind will thank you for it.

Most of all, remember that Paleo is a choice. A choice based on giving your body the nourishment that it evolved to expect; pure and simple. As you thrive, you will learn to love Paleo more with every passing week. Have fun, stay positive and let this exceptional way of looking after your body carry you into a much brighter future.

12573938R00044

Printed in Poland
by Amazon Fulfillment
Poland Sp. z o.o., Wrocław